August '79
to Dear Ted
with memory
and anticipation—
[illegible] ane

The Sea in Their Blood

The Sea in Their Blood

Frederick John Pratson

Illustrated with photographs by the author

Houghton Mifflin Company Boston 1972

FIRST PRINTING H

ISBN: 0-395-13652-0
LIBRARY OF CONGRESS CATALOG CARD NUMBER: 79-177531
PRINTED IN THE UNITED STATES OF AMERICA

TO MY WIFE, PATRICIA

"All past civilizations have offered choices to men. Ideas have been exchanged, along with technological innovations, but never on so vast, overwhelming, and single-directed a scale as in the present. Increasingly, there is but one way into the future: the technological way. The frightening aspect of this situation lies in the constriction of human choice."

LOREN EISELEY
The unexpected Universe

Acknowledgments

My travels have taken me along the coasts of Maine, in the United States, Nova Scotia, New Brunswick, and the north coast of Quebec, in eastern Canada. Each community I visited was distinctive in its own special way. If I were to list the names of all the people in the United States and in Canada who were helpful to me, it would take up several pages of this book. I want to use this occasion to express my deep appreciation for their friendship and hope that this effort confirms their faith in me. In addition, I am particularly grateful to the following individuals without whose friendship and encouragement this book would not be possible: Father Ernest Sweeny, Mr. Paul Coolidge, The Reverend Robert Bryan, Miss Josephine Rogers, Mr. Richard McAdoo, Mrs. Arabel Porter, and my wife, Patricia.

Contents

Introduction

The way of life portrayed in this book is one that has been shaped by the environment of the sea, generation after generation. These (inshore) fishing people, of the state of Maine and of the provinces of Nova Scotia, New Brunswick and the north coast of Quebec, possess qualities of courage, self-reliance, rugged independence, and human kindness to a degree which have become, for many, nostalgic myths of the past. It is a surprise to find communities of people who live in relative peace and harmony, a harmony strengthened by the many dangers of their way of work which frequently brings them pain and grief.

One finds here distinct cultural differences, such as between the Scots and the French Acadians of Nova Scotia or between the Yankees of Maine and the English-speaking fishermen of the north coast of Quebec. We can experience these differences in the way the people look, talk, worship, cook, and celebrate. The Nova Scotia Scot, for example, still likes to put on his highland games and occasionally wears his kilts and blows on his bagpipes. The New Brunswick French Acadian still enjoys his Gallic and his garlic, and remembers the history of his people through the tale of a lovely young lady, Evangeline. The Maritime Loyalist's heart continues to warm more toward the Union Jack and "God Save the Queen" rather than toward the red-and-white maple leaf flag and "Oh Canada." And the Maine Yankee is as taciturn as ever, a unique species among all the people on the earth. But as impressive as are these differences, it is the commonality of their struggles, hopes and disappointments that bind these various peoples together.

I have come to admire the maritime people of Maine and eastern Canada and have created this book for them and for all people who are inspired by the triumph of the human spirit over great odds. My hope is that this book does not become an obituary of a way of life but rather serves as a stimulus to its renaissance.

Frederick John Pratson
North Scituate, Mass.
Summer, 1971

Lessons from the Sea

I stood on the granite ledges of Peggy's Cove, Nova Scotia, and felt the force of a fierce wind and sea around me.

I was an uneasy alien in a strange place, somewhere where only gods and fishermen dared to laugh at a violent nature.

The people who live on the coasts of Maine and eastern Canada can trace their lineage to some of the earliest settlers of the North American continent: Indians, French, Germans, English, Scots, Portuguese. Their roots are well nourished on past events of adventure, exploration, war and the establishment of European civilization in the Western Hemisphere. Theirs is also the epic struggle of man against the sea. Part of their destiny is the result of the romance of history; part is the remarkable reality of their continuum despite all forms of economic, political, social, and environmental hardships. In their faces you can see the imprint of their backgrounds; the twinkling eyes of an Irishman or the determined chin of a Yankee. Theirs is a multiplicity of origins that has evolved now into an unmistakable singleness of spirit.

Their way of life is not for the soft, the protected, or the cowardly. It is a way of life that clings to its rock-based communities like crusty barnacles rooted there for generations, refusing to be swept aside by the constant onslaught of a harsh and unrelenting sea or the tides of man's changing ways.

Unlike the men who work as crews on the large draggers and trawlers which stay out as long as is needed to fill their holds, the individual inshore fisherman works his day out at sea, usually returning to his home port in the late afternoon. Lobstering, for example, is a typical inshore fishing activity. The use of weirs, a method of fishing learned from the Indians, is another. Along the north coast of Quebec, net traps are constructed close to the shoreline to trap schools of seals which swim by in winter and early spring.

"The inshore fisherman is one who goes out to sea every morning but hurries home each night to the bed of his wife. He's always got one foot on land and the other in his boat." However, there are many times when he sails far beyond the sight of land, working in his boat as long as there is fair weather and fish to be caught. Unlike many draggermen, he is his own master, managing his craft and life as he pleases, experiencing every day both the beauty and cruelty of the sea, often alone and with a sense of freedom.

To understand the inshore fishing people of Maine and eastern Canada and their way of life one must listen to what the sea has taught them, teachings they recount in their own words of lessons won sometimes at the price of life itself. This is a quality of knowledge that is ingrained in the man who does not merely walk the shoreline, who does not put out to sea for a pleasurable interlude or seek to harvest it from some factory ship. Singly or in the company of a few he works every daylight hour, or night time if need be, of the fishing season, wresting from the sea not only what feeds the body but that which nourishes in the process his soul.

"I love the sea and take it as a friend. It's something to watch the sea get real angry. When it blows all you can do is hang on to the gunwale and watch it kick up a hell of a mess around you. It can be terrible and lonely. You bounce around the water like a cork gone crazy and you wonder if the next wave is the one that'll smash you and your boat to pieces. And, then, all of a sudden the sea calms down and you wonder to yourself how everything so ugly one minute can be so beautiful the next. It's then that you think about all the good fellows that were killed and about the loss of your gear and the damage to the boat. But, even with all the bad things that have happened, you really can't hate the sea because you depend so much upon it."

"We've been making a living out of fishing for generations. You're either good at it or you're bad. The good ones survive and the bad ones are either warming their behinds on land or they're dead. There's no mystery to this business. It's a lot of plain hard work, luck, and a need to live the best you can from one day to the next."

"Most of the time you're out at sea all by yourself. It helps a great deal if you like your own company."

"We don't fear the sea, but we sure respect it. The sea demands that you use good judgment all the time. Most of the time there isn't a second chance to correct a bad mistake. You've got to be ready all the time. When you go out many miles at sea, you sometimes see a boat break up and men drown. You can't keep worrying about men drowning in bad weather. You talk over what went wrong and the next day you go out again. You don't quit. You just keep going."

"There's nothing like three or four good fellows working together out at sea . . . nothing like it in the world."

"I was sailing a two-sticker, off of the Grand Banks not far from the coast of Newfoundland, when I saw a thresher and a swordfish take on a whale. The thresher was on top of the whale and swordfish was on the bottom. They sure were churning up the water with foam and blood . . . but it wasn't long before they got the whale and it was all over for him. It sure was a beautiful sight to see that thresher and swordfish working together against that whale."

"It's not so much a question of what the boat will take out at sea . . . but one of how much can the man take."

"This business of fishing for a living is a constant challenge. And all of us have a gambler's hope of making a killing and coming out of it real rich.

"On the other hand, you've got to be prepared to be wiped out. When the sea gets angry, it can destroy everything you've got, your boat, shed, wharf, and gear. If that happens, you've got to make a decision to either go on or quit for good. It happened to me during a hurricane several years ago. I decided to stick with it. Maybe I was a bit off my rocker to go on . . . but, I guess, I can't do anything else as well as fish for a living. Once you've got the sea in your blood, you're hooked to it for good."

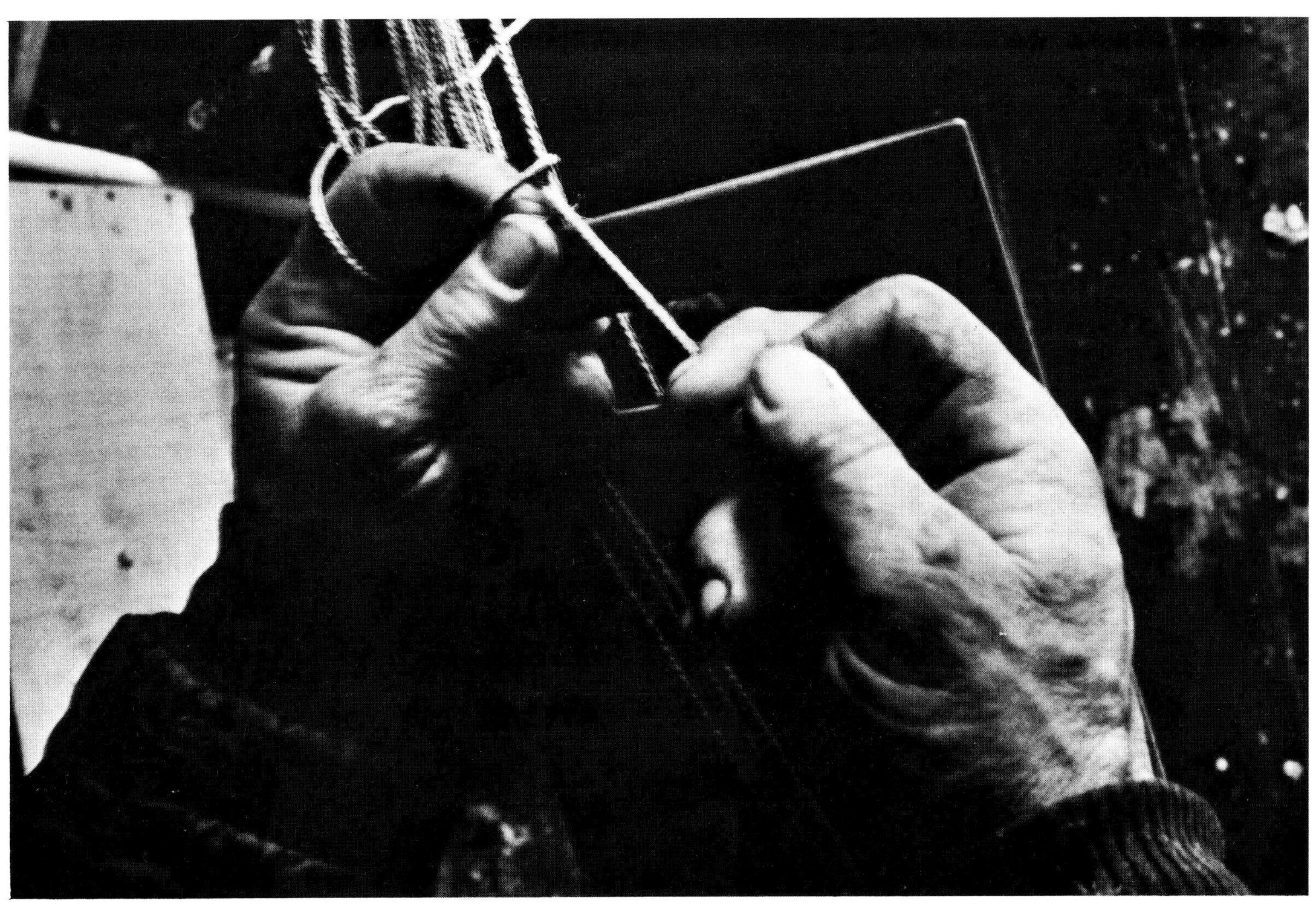

"There are so many things that can go wrong or come up unexpected out at sea. We make sure that all we know about this business is under control, and we hope and pray that when something difficult or new hits us we'll be able to handle it. Many a boat and its crew get into trouble because the things they should've cared for back in port, but forgot or neglected, take their attentions from some more serious dangers, and they end up hurt or on the bottom."

"One thing that a man has to watch for is his own greed. He has to be careful not to take in his boat more than the sea will allow."

The sea gives a living to the people and it takes a few of them in return. It has always been that way and the people accept the reality that both man and the sea will have their victories. Hardly anyone who works the sea speaks of courage or glorifies this quality because without courage they would not be there.

A Man's Man

I saw in that leathery-faced man of the sea what I always wanted to be. He created a world with strength from his hands and back, while I could only conjure one in my mind. His world could be seen, touched, smelled, and tasted. Mine was but a dream of vanishing images.

This man from Harrington Harbour, Quebec, is a man's man. His life is not for those who are weak or lazy. He is an expert mariner, fisherman, sealer, trapper, hunter, storyteller, family man and citizen. He can fix what goes wrong in his house or out at sea. He is his own boss and master of his own time. He also shares with most inshore fishermen courage, self-reliance, mastery of various crafts, good judgment and an adventurous spirit. He is one of a breed of men who are rare in a more sophisticated society but who can be readily found along the rugged northeastern coasts. The survival of their families, communities, and way of life depends on their being what they are, and nothing less.

"The thing I like best about fishing for a living is that I'm my own boss. Nobody tells me what to do or how to do it."

"A lot of my gear was passed on to me by my father. But I've had to put several thousands of dollars of my own and some from the bank into new equipment and a better boat. You know, you can't use the same kind of gear for lobster that you use for herring. For lobster you need special traps, buoys and lines. And for herring you need a seine so that the little sardines won't get away. And when you go after cod or mackerel, you need larger nets or trawling lines. All of this costs a pretty penny. Sometimes more than we can afford."

"I'm up before dawn and out baiting and hauling my lobster pots when most people are still in bed. And it's more often than not that I'm still working when the same people are getting ready to go to sleep again."

Beals Island people in Maine, now connected with Jonesport by a steel bridge, take pride in building good lobster boats. It's a craft that sons learn from their fathers. It is not unusual to pass by a Beals Island house and see sitting next to it, secure in its supports, a lobster boat in the process of being built. On the deck is a father who is fitting in a plank with his son beside him, helping his father to hold and position the wood. Beals Island sons learn by doing and, after a while, building a good lobster boat becomes almost as natural as baiting and hauling a day's worth of lobster pots.

While no fisherman can make exclusive claim to any part of the sea, those waters which are immediately adjacent to a particular community are, by long custom, considered to be territory belonging to the men of that town or village. This sense of territory becomes more important during the lucrative lobster season. These territories, of course, overlap each other but the men know and respect the extreme limits. They also know that interloping can work both ways. The open sea, on the other hand, is a different matter. There a man's territory is where his net, trawl, or traps happen to be. Once he leaves a good fishing spot, that area can be freely used by anyone who happens to come along.

While the inshore fisherman knows intimately the coastline of his area and carries most of this knowledge in his head, there are many times when he must rely on what others have provided to help him when he is in unfamiliar waters, in fog, or in an angry sea. The coastline of Maine and eastern Canada has been charted, as have other parts of the coast, with great detail to help provide accurate navigation for mariners. Lighthouses, buoys, horns, and other markers warn of dangers, such as rocks and shoals. They also serve as navigational aids. Meteorological stations, the U.S. Coast Guard, Royal Canadian Mounted Police coastal patrols, and U.S. and Canadian naval patrols (both surface and air) provide the fisherman with information on weather and sea conditions and help him when he is in distress.

"We were in a fog one day that was so thick I couldn't see my bow. I managed to get myself started from one buoy, setting my compass to where I figured was another. I got home that day by dead reckoning, from buoy to buoy. If it wasn't for those markers, I'd still be out there."

Competition from foreign fishing fleets, Federal government indifference, harassment on the high seas, excessive insurance rates, oil spillage, mercury poisoning, changing habits of marine life — all present difficult odds against which the inshore fishermen must battle. The payoff for their labors is uncertain and their economic future often looks bleak. This condition exists not only for fishing people living on the coasts of Maine and eastern Canada but on all the coasts of North America.

"I'm out as long as the fish are biting. You can't predict what the fish will do from one day to the next. You can get several thousand pounds one day and make a good bundle . . . and go out the next only to find that the fish have gone. The fish seem smarter these days. It's almost as if they had college educations. It's very hard to get ahead in this business. Sometimes it's hard just to stay even."

The bearded old man from Lubec, Maine, is in the business of building and repairing boats. He says he's the best darn boat builder and fixer he knows. He has enough confidence in his craftsmanship to go out onto the bay in one of his latest creations. His shop is a crazy quilt of just about everything one could ever imagine, an antique shop and junkyard all rolled into one. It's one of the very few places in Lubec where one can find the bleached skull of a cow. The black son of a mangy Persian feline has free rein over the entire place, except on the woodwork of one of the boats being made in the shop. If out of a moment of unconscious stupidity the cat should leap from its favorite resting spot — a shelf full of Mason jars of nails — and land on the raw wood gunwale of the dory, the old man's fist of three stout fingers and two stumps will come down on the unfortunate creature and send it off like an interstellar comet to the rusty toes of a nearby Franklin stove. But except for that one strict rule, almost anything can live in peace with the craftsman from Lubec.

At about four o'clock in the afternoon, in the little fishing village of Terence Bay, Nova Scotia, those men who have come back from sea, sold their catches, and have taken care of their gear begin coming into the fishing shed. It's a rough-beamed structure, hardly large enough to hold the eight men sitting on crates or on the rumble seat of a long-forgotten jalopy. There is also a napping hound sprawled near a potbelly stove and about ten thousand objects ranging from nets to nails to ice skates.

The men wear boots and overalls. One puts on his sou-wester hat just because he likes the feel of it. The hat is one of the most universal symbols of what he is, a seafaring man. A bottle of Demarara rum is making the rounds, just enough to relax and mellow, and the stove is radiating a warm heat that makes eyelids heavy and minds turn to sleep. The men talk about sea disasters, from the *Atlantic* in the 1800s to that of the more recent *Cape Bonnie,* which went down off their Nova Scotia rocks.

They talk about the current market for their catches and about the latest gossip of the village. One of the young men feels like singing and his baritone voice brings forth tales of loyalty, love, and the sea, making everyone in the shed journey into his own memory to remember and to feel. After the singing and another round of rum, this time from the bootlegger, a calendar of nude girls is taken down from some remote hiding place in the attic and a widower turns the pages slowly, saying, "Nothing to get excited about, boys. Just a lot of colored paint on paper. Nothing to get excited about."

At the point when the colored paint on paper starts to look like real flesh and blood, a woman's voice is heard calling from the outside. "It's my woman. Must be suppertime," says one of the men who has been sleeping near the stove. The others look at their watches and one by one they leave.

"Me and my two buddies were many miles out into the Atlantic. We had already put eight tubs of trawl over the side when Billy managed to get one of the nasty hooks into the palm of his hand. He acted so frightened and excited that we thought that the poor fellow would die on the spot . . . and so did Billy. Poor Billy hollered at me to get him back to home port so that a doctor could fix his hand. I would have done that . . . but with all that trawl out and the fish start'n to grab at the bait . . . it just didn't make sense to go home just to fix Billy's hand. I told Billy to grab hold of the starboard gunwale with his good hand and I took his hurt one in mine. The hook wasn't far in but to Billy it was the same as hav'n a swordfish harpoon deep in his heart. To me it looked like it was only, what I'd call, pierc'n the lip of a cod. So I took my gutt'n knife and in hardly a second I sliced through that nice pink flesh of Billy's hand and took out the hook as clean as a whistle. Why, Billy didn't even know it was out until I made him look at it. Everyth'n was go'n well to that moment . . . but it was the look'n that really did it to Billy. He saw the blood dripp'n toward his wrist. The next th'n I knew, Marty, my other partner, was holler'n at me: 'Billy's go'n over the side!' And there he was, faint'n dead away and flipp'n himself over the starboard side. Well . . . we got to him just before his bald head touched the sea. That poor Billy . . . he's a good fisherman . . . but he never could stand the sight of blood."

"When we're not fishing, the thing we like best to do is hunt . . . caribou, moose, deer, rabbits, all kinds of birds. It helps to put some different kind of meat on the table. You get to look forward to a good feed of deer or wild goose. But, most of all, we just like to hunt. I would go so far as to say that there probably isn't a man or boy, who's from a fishing family, who doesn't like to hunt. It would seem kind of unnatural if he didn't."

Cherry Valley
TOMATOES

I had finished eating a big feed of thick rabbit stew, homemade bread, apple pie, rum, and tea. A wood-burning stove and my thick Irish fisherman's sweater kept me snug and warm. The house we were in sat on a remote ledge overlooking the Gulf of St. Lawrence. We were far from what most people would call civilization, but we were also at the very center of the universe.

The Sea in Her Blood

I could see in her all the ages of life, from an infant to that of an old woman.

I could see the fresh innocence of a new bride, unquestioning in a worn photograph, and now the tired, illusion-free mother and wife, resigned to the present reality.

I saw in all her ages a changing, maturing beauty and a growing strength.

I saw in her my mother, my daughter, and my wife.

Life for seacoast women revolves almost totally around that of child rearing and homemaking. Most have resigned themselves to what their husbands have done with their lives, such as this herring fisherman's wife from a Bay of Fundy village in New Brunswick: "I suppose if there was a choice, I would like to have my husband do another kind of work. Something that is not quite so hard . . . so dangerous . . . and so discouraging in terms of money. But there's nothing else to do except for fishing . . . if you want to live in these parts."

"I would be very happy if our son did not follow his father into fishing. I would hate to see him and the girl he marries go through the same disappointments we've had to face. Every year of our marriage we said to ourselves that the next year would be a better one. But life seems to go on pretty much as before. Nothing has really changed that much. I pray that there's something more to look forward to for our son."

WORLD'S

"Every afternoon, while I'm peeling potatoes for supper, I stand by the kitchen window and wait for the first sight of his boat. When I see its bow coming in around the bend in the rocks, I can relax because he is safe. Sometimes the time goes past when he said he would be home . . . and I get a terrible sick feeling that lasts until he comes in or one of the other men tells me that he's all right and will be in a little late. So far, he hasn't been seriously hurt. But a friend of mine, who lives on the other side of the village, lost her man over a month ago in a storm. It happens to us people all the time . . . and I wonder, every time when he goes out to sea, if this is the time it will happen to us."

"My husband was a man of the sea. I read once where they called men like him iron men who went out on wooden ships. He was like that. And he made a good life for me and my children before he got drowned, over twenty-five years ago, when his boat got smashed in a storm. I'm proud of being a widow woman . . . because I'm as proud of him today as I was when he was alive."

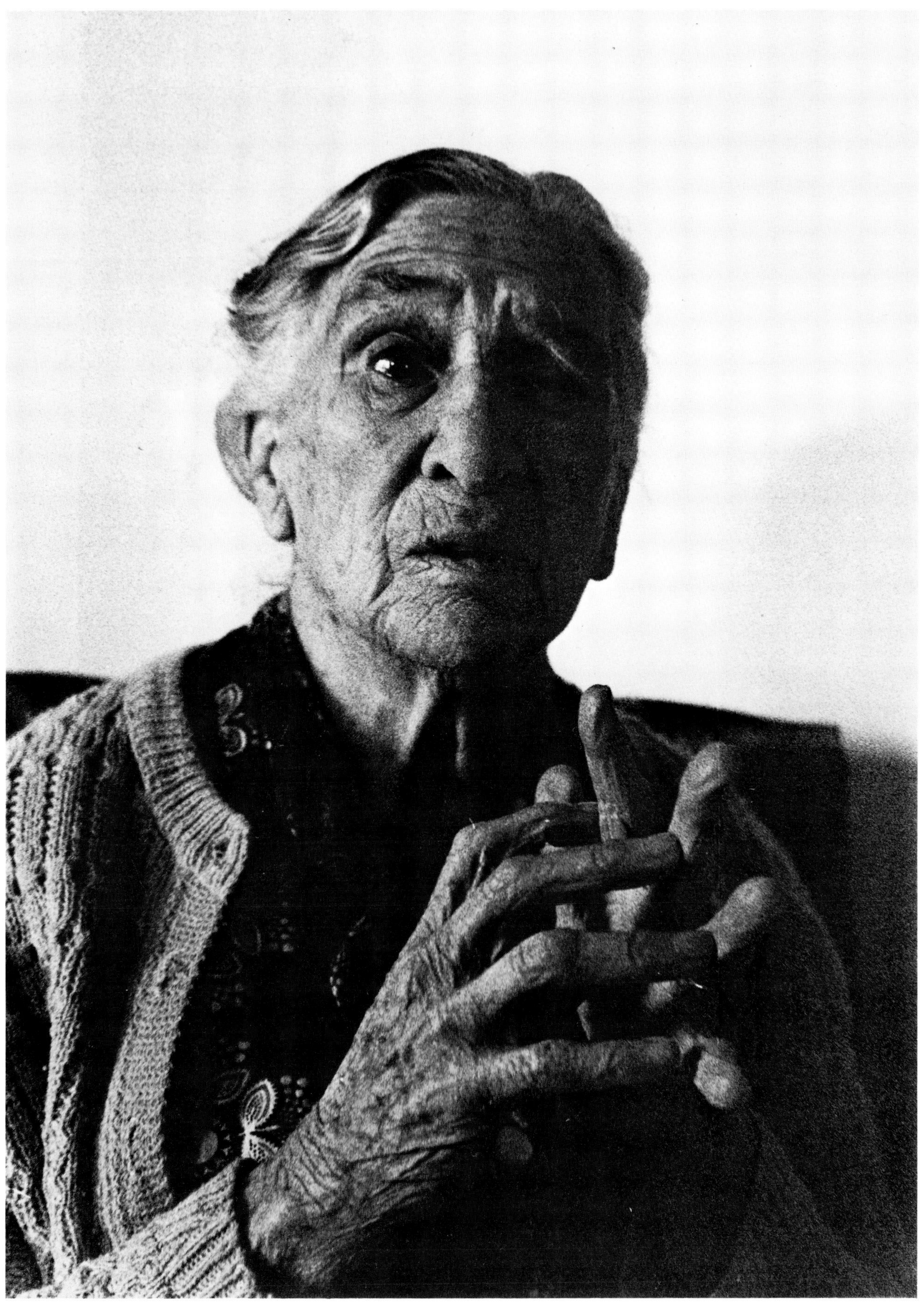

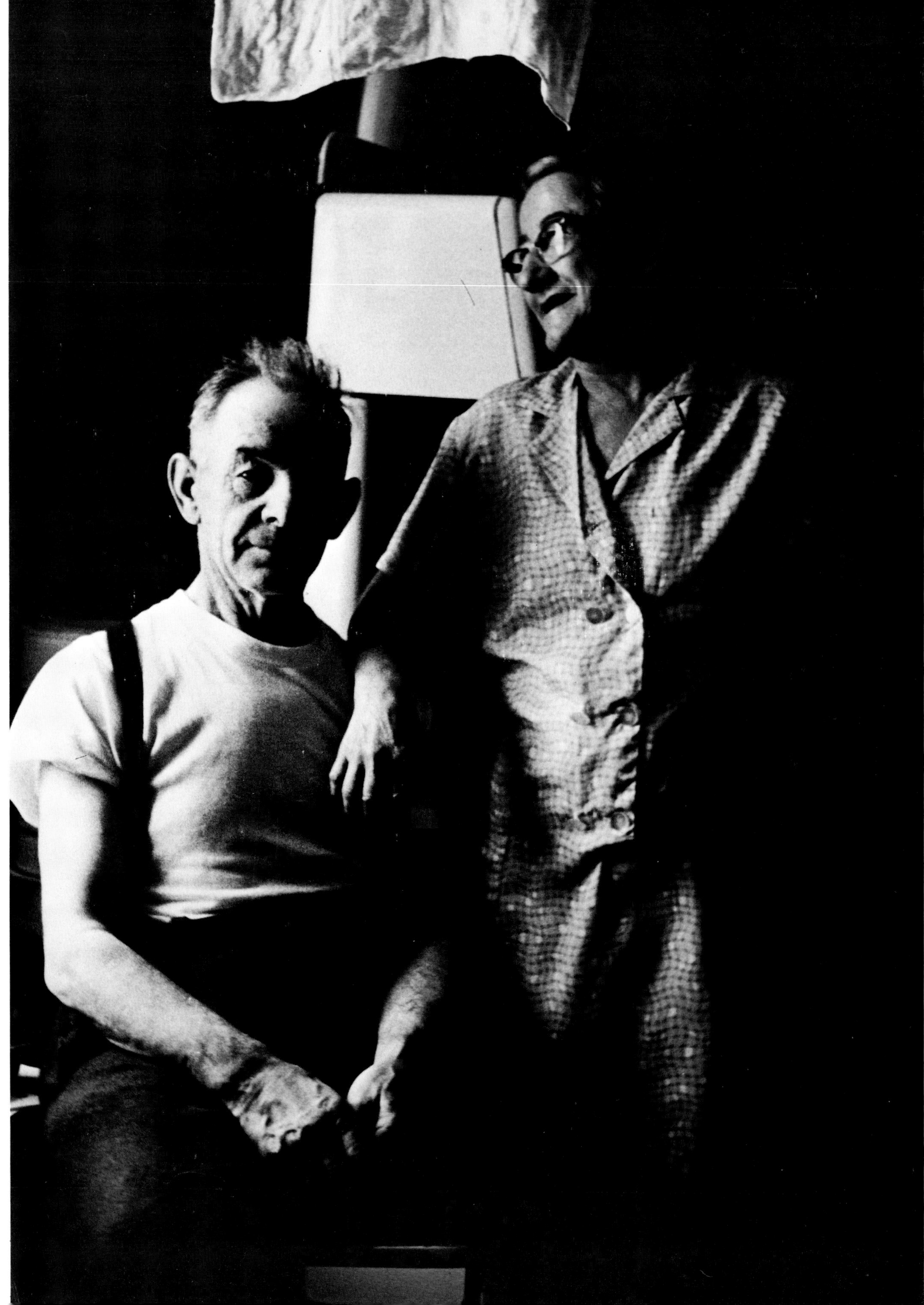

"My husband loves the sea and fishing," says a Maine woman. "I can't think of him doing anything else. There's not many times when he isn't thinking, talking or reading about fishing, even when we go on a vacation. When we go on vacation, he doesn't want to go to the big cities, like Boston or New York. He says that they're just too confusing, dirty, and expensive. What he likes to do is to visit other fishing towns, like Gloucester in Massachusetts or up to Lunenburg in Nova Scotia, and see the way they do things there. He says that just because it's a vacation that's no reason to spend all your time in loafing . . . some of the time should be spent learning. While I'd like for us to have some more money, so as to take some of the worry out of life, I can't say we're unhappy with the way we live. Our families have always lived off of the sea. It would be hard to think of us doing something different. In fact, the way the rest of the world is going, sometimes I think that we're not so bad off after all."

A mother is concerned with the future of her daughter. She knows that a woman's security and fulfillment, if she continues to live on the coast, is within a family, the one she was born into and the one she will create on her own.

From a hilltop in a fishing village overlooking Passamaquoddy Bay I watched a young woman as she came out of her house. Her face was pretty and wholesome and her well-developed breasts and hips were those of a mature woman, ripe for the pleasures of love and the task of bearing children. Childhood lasts long enough in such villages but not too long, and unmarried girls who turn twenty usually begin to wonder if life is passing them by. I watched her as she tried to consume the time that hung heavy from one moment to another by pacing in front of her house, striking provocative poses, enticing unseen, imaginary lovers. Finally a battered pickup truck, with a loose muffler churning the road dirt, came around a curve and stopped in front of her. A young man opened the truck's door for her and she slipped in close beside him. They kissed each other with great passion and then drove off, spinning a thick cloud of dust after them. The curtains in a front window of the house parted and an older woman's face came into view. She pressed her cheek against the glass pane, trying to catch sight of the truck, before she saw me watching her and pulled the curtains closed.

"My God!" says an Acadian fisherman. "What am I going to do? Six daughters!

"I have six daughters and all the young men are moving to the cities. There's no jobs for them here, except for fishing. And they don't want to put up with one good season one year and a bad one the next. The Russians and the other foreign countries, with their big factory ships, are fishing the hell out of our water, and there's nothing left for us, much less any young man who wants to support a new wife and later some kids. If only a big company would come in and open up a plant around here. That would keep the boys from moving. I don't like the idea of having to come up with six doweries . . . but that's better than having all six of them staying at home."

Our Way of Life

I have never been in this village before but I feel that I can belong and call it home.

"It was quite a fierce storm that night and the *Cape Bonnie* was last reported just outside of Halifax. But that position was a mistake. Search parties went out looking for her in the wrong place. That boat went down off of the rocks outside of this harbor, Terence Bay. All of her hands were lost. When we found her the next day, every able man and boy from this village went out and recovered all the dead bodies, except for two which we couldn't find. No one asked us to do this. And, as far as I can tell, no one from the company ever thanked us."

SHEILA·LYNN
SYD
SYD
NS

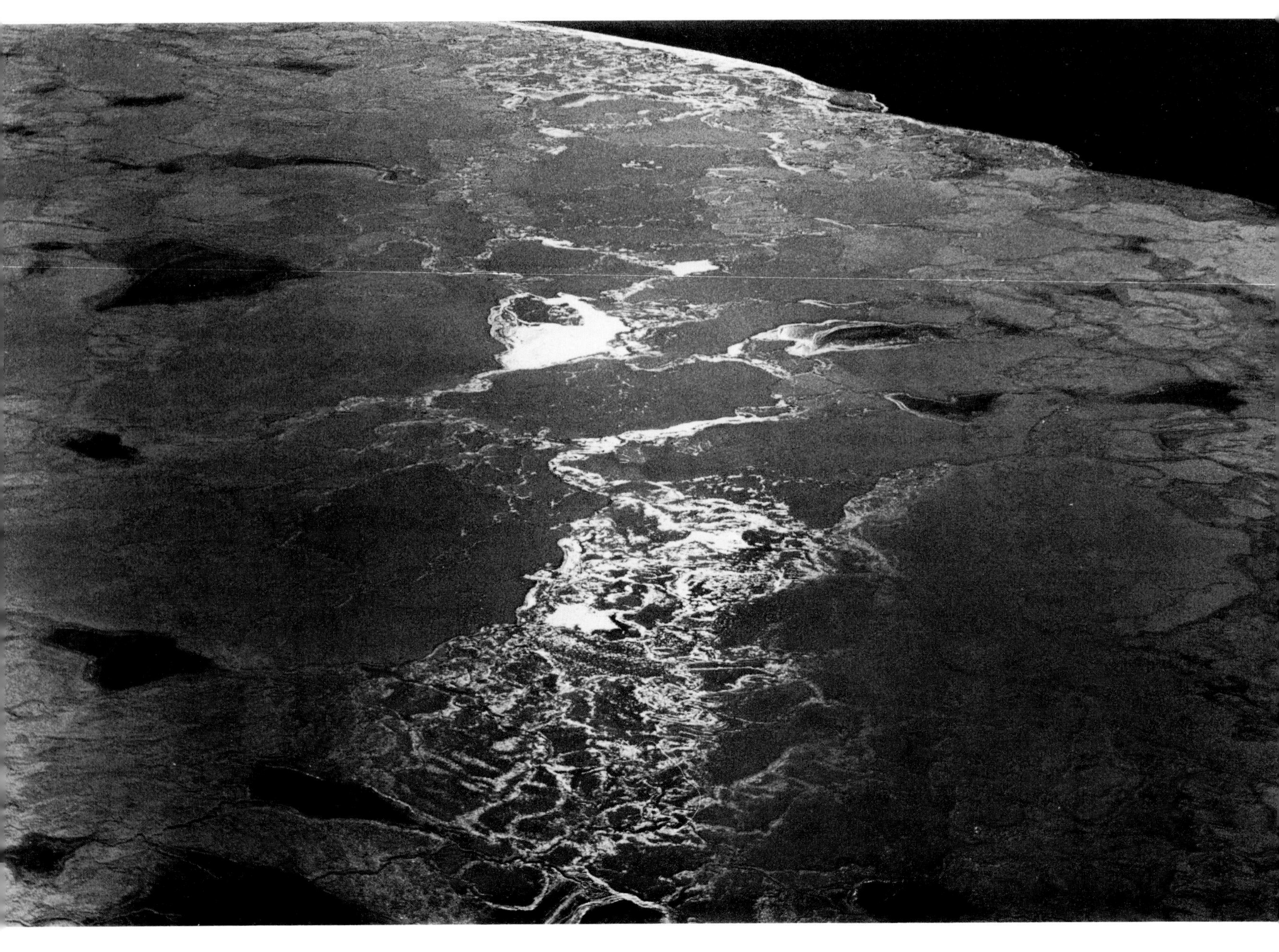

"We wouldn't think of paying someone to do for us what we can do for ourselves. We don't have the time and the money to hire out our work. Besides, we get a real kick, you might say, out of doing things ourselves and not depending on somebody else. It's a good feeling to know that you can build a more sea-worthy boat or do a better job at lobstering than another fellow. That's a kind of feeling no man can take away from you."

Because the individual is frequently isolated when he is out at sea or deep in the bush, the people have developed a system of keeping in touch with each other so that a man may have a better chance of survival if he finds himself in trouble. It is part of the daily ritual for a fisherman to tell his wife and some of the other men where he is going and the time he will be back. If he goes to another community by boat, snowmobile, dog sled or auto, he lets people at both ends know the time of his arrival and the route he is taking. Many lives have been saved out at sea or in the back-country wilderness because search parties have known when to go out and where to look. "Did you see him?" "What was he doing?" "Is he all right?" "Does he need help?"

"I built me own boat and I built me own home. I do most of the repairing around here, too. Now there are some kinds of jobs that I'm not as handy at as another fellar, like electrical wiring. If I have a problem with me wiring, I just call my friend Henry, who knows how to take care of those things real well. Henry used to work for an electrician in St. John, you know. Well, Henry comes to my house and helps me fix me problem. Except for giving him a drink or two of rum, that's if I have some in the house at the time, I don't pay Henry a dime . . . and Henry don't expect it. Now if Henry has some trouble with that 1935 Ford engine he's got to power his boat, Henry knows he can count on me to help him. But it isn't that way just between Henry and me, every man, woman and child around here knows they can count on each other when they need help. That's the way it is here or when you're out at sea. Sometimes there be a man or a woman who won't help someone who needs it. That person is just hurting themself because people won't be around when he needs help. But there's not too many of that kind around here. You know, I like doing what I can by myself, but it's good to know you've got some friends when you need them."

In Nova Scotia they tell the story of two bachelor brothers who caught lobsters like mad during the season. After selling their catches, they spent all their money on bootleg rum. When they needed more rum, they went ahead and sold their gear and also their boat to get more money. After they drank that down, they borrowed money to buy some more.

On and on it went, the same routine every season. Still the brothers made a point of paying off their debts and earning enough money to buy new gear and a new boat. And when the season started again anew, so did they. The brothers were kind of strange, living all by themselves, never bothering to get married, and never letting anyone into their house. One day, the parish priest came to their home to see if they were all right because people in the village had not seen them for several days. The priest came into the house and found one brother stone drunk from rum and talking to the other brother who had been dead for over three days. The brother who had died was over ninety and the other was eighty-six.

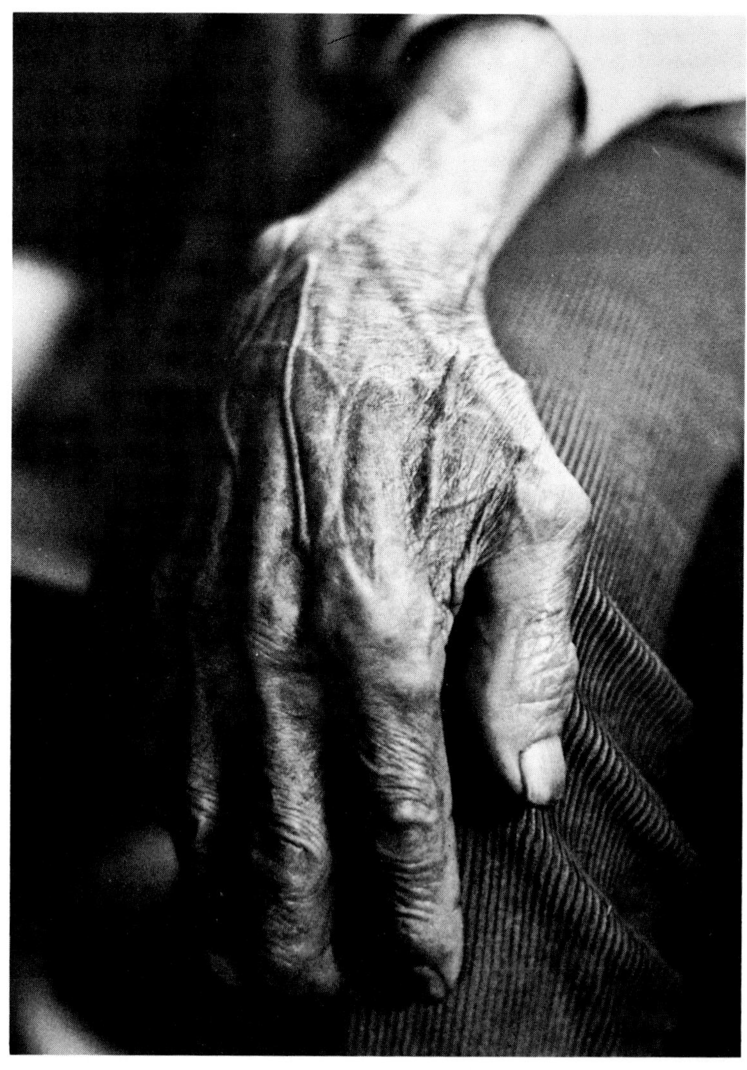

The cats at Prospect Harbour, Nova Scotia, are everywhere. A fisherman cuts a live dogfish that continues to wriggle even when it is in a half a dozen separate parts on the dock. The cats attack the squirming sections and sink their sharp teeth into the bloody flesh, making deep-throated growls as they tear away and devour. "The cats keep the rats under control. If it wasn't for the cats our nets and gear would be ruined by the rats. And if it wasn't for the cats, the rats might soon drive all us people out of our village."

While more manufactured products are being made available to even the remotest communities, there are many individuals who continue to work at handicrafts because it is a good way to spend time when bad weather and off-season conditions free them from work and because they have a love of making something beautiful with their hands. Many of the people are natural artists, demonstrating through their crafts a keen sense of taste in sculpture, painting, and textiles. In almost every community one can find a man who carves figurines out of soft pine, people and animals, or makes toys for children, such as sleds and small boats. The women hook rugs and mats and weave fabrics of complex patterns and colors. Along the north coast of Quebec, for example, the women make stuffed animal toys, using unborn seal fur for the soft, white outer covering. The designs the people use in making their crafts are part of their lives.

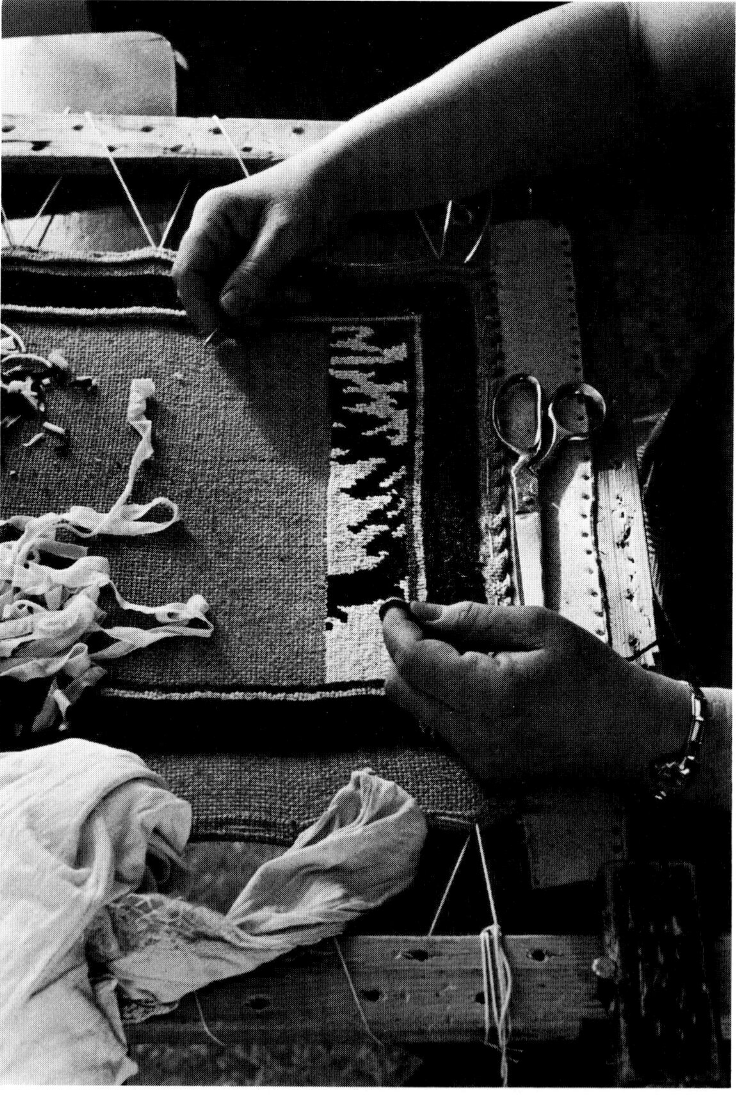

Lindsays Slaunwhite house caught fire Nov 9th 1933
Royal Hotel Burned Down on awful cold night Dec 29 1933
Zachariahs Jollimores House burned down Nov 4 th 1934
Robert Slaunwhite seine got 16½ thousand of mackeral
Eastern Berth woody Island
George Drew got 50 Barrels of mackeral
Jeremiah Slaunwhite got 75 Barells mackeral Nov 4th 1934
Govt Steamer Aranmore anchored in Terence Bay
2 days trying to replace buoys Feby 16th 1937
Big storm all the nets lost and Light house had shingles ripped off. and a Big rock fell down in Lewis Cove Sept 26th 1937
Big storm lots of nets lost and Schooner
S S Lunenburg wind south East Oct 24 1938
Pilot Boat Hebridean was sunk in a collision with a Newfoundland Freighter 6 men drowned & 10 rescued at Pilot Boat Station Hfx Harbour Mch 28th 1940
high tide and storm lot of stages went down

"We've had many shipwrecks around these parts of Nova Scotia. One we still talk about is when the steamship *Atlantic,* from the United States, went down in 1873. Five hundred and seventy-seven persons lost their lives but there were more than two hundred survivors. It was a rough sea that day. The *Atlantic* hit her bow on some rocks and then her stern swung at more rocks and then she layed out on her side. A woman was making bread in this house when she saw some of the survivors coming up the road. When they came in they were so hungry that they ate all the raw dough. And they were so soaking wet that holes had to be bored in the floor to let the water run out. The dead ones were buried in the Catholic and Protestant cemeteries in our village. It was a terrible thing but people around here still remember the *Atlantic* and they still talk about her."

"When a couple gets married, all the men show up in their Sunday best, toting their shotguns. During the celebration, the men get together and they shoot off their guns in the air. Well, it can get kind of dangerous, especially when there's been a lot of drinking and folks are feeling good. The men still bring their shotguns to the weddings, but they don't shoot them off like they once did because the ministers and the police are scared at what might happen. You know, it's a shame. It was a real nice way of feeling happy but now it's just about gone."

"There are some among us, though not many to be sure, who want to be 'highliners' at any cost. They steal from our lobster traps. They take our gear and try to make a killing at our expense. But they're soon found out. And then life gets difficult for them. If such a person comes from our village, he soon finds out that people won't talk to him or help him when he needs it. Everywhere he goes he'll know that someone is watching him and that he's not to be trusted and that no one likes him. Before long he'll find that he's all by himself and he knows he can't wait it out because we never forget. Then there's nothing for him to do but to get out before he starves or gets hurt. Now if he's from some other village, we tell his people and they usually treat him pretty much as we would. A dishonest man hurts everyone, especially himself and his family. Our life is too hard to afford that kind of man."

Fishing communities in Maine and eastern Canada are perched on cliffs or ledges facing the sea. The plain but sturdy wood frame houses are usually scattered on different levels of flat areas and ridges in contrast to the regimentation of many suburban developments. Many have an informal system of paths, roads, trails, boardwalks, or bridges that connect various parts of a community into a comprehensible whole, offering open space, scenic vistas, human scale, and rapid intimacy with everywhere.

If you go to Blandford, Nova Scotia, you can still see whales being brought in and processed into canned meat, oil, and fertilizer. In Lubec, Maine, you can smell herring being smoked until they become kippered. Stonington, Maine, men bring in some of the best cold-water lobsters available anywhere on this earth. And in Blacks Harbour, New Brunswick, you can see, smell, and taste sardines being packed into almost every conceivable kind of sauce.

"Many times strangers come here and it ain't long before they be leav'n and say'n that we're not friendly. Well, that ain't so. It's just that we kind of like to take our time with them and sometimes we just plain have a hard time show'n that we're friendly."

"The strangers are on the docks when we pull in. They try to be friendly with us because they think we'll give them some free fish or a lower price than what they'd pay for in a market. Sometimes we play along with them, like we would a lively salmon with a hook deep in his mouth. Most of the time we're too darn busy and tired to pay any attention to them. Sometimes a stranger does come along who really knows how to talk to us. And if he brings along a bottle of rum to share with us, he can go home with all the fish he can carry."

"We get a lot of tourists and summer people and they're not here more than a day or two before they want to change everything around to please them. It comes as a real shock to them when they find out that they're the ones that's got to change, not us."

"A lot of outsiders are coming into our town and looking at us and our ways. Sometimes, we put on a kind of show for them and when they go away we go back to being what we really are like. But maybe someday we won't be able to go back and, then, we'll have to live the show."

"A stranger is always welcome to share the food at my table. It may not be what he's used to . . . but it's what me and the family eats. And, as I say, he's welcome to join us. If he's caught in our village for the night, he can count on sleeping in a warm bed. Almost everyone who lives along this coast would do the same for a traveler . . . if he's someone they know or a stranger. When we go to another village, we know we can expect the same."

"Before the television came in, I used to go to the general store, up the hill, every evening to play cards with my buddies. We used to play every five cents like it was a thousand-dollar bill. Now nobody goes to the store to play cards anymore because we're all home watching television. We don't visit each other and talk like we used to because of the television."

In those remote villages, such as Harrington Harbour, Quebec, where there is no television as yet, people have time to talk and visit. When there is a community affair, such as a combination buffet dinner, fashion show, and dance, it starts around five in the afternoon and reluctantly ends at five or six the next morning. The entire community attends as well as people from neighboring villages, some of whom come long distances by boat in the summer and snowmobile in the winter.

The dinner offered almost every kind of meat, fish, vegetable, relish, bread and sweets, served by the local women dressed in Dutch costumes which they had made themselves. A new group of eaters came into the hall every few minutes and the food never seemed to run out. A potent homemade brew was changing hands outside in the bitter cold and a few got more than just a party glow. After several hours of the dinner, the fashion show began and the minister's wife introduced the models. Even grandmothers came gliding down the ramp. For comic relief, two men dressed themselves as women and their antics brought down the house. Then the dance started and it kept going until a new day's sun crept over a horizon of polar ice. Though everyone was exhausted, many talked about the wedding that was going to take place in a few days in the next village and of the fun that would start all over again.

Upon This Rock I Will Build My House

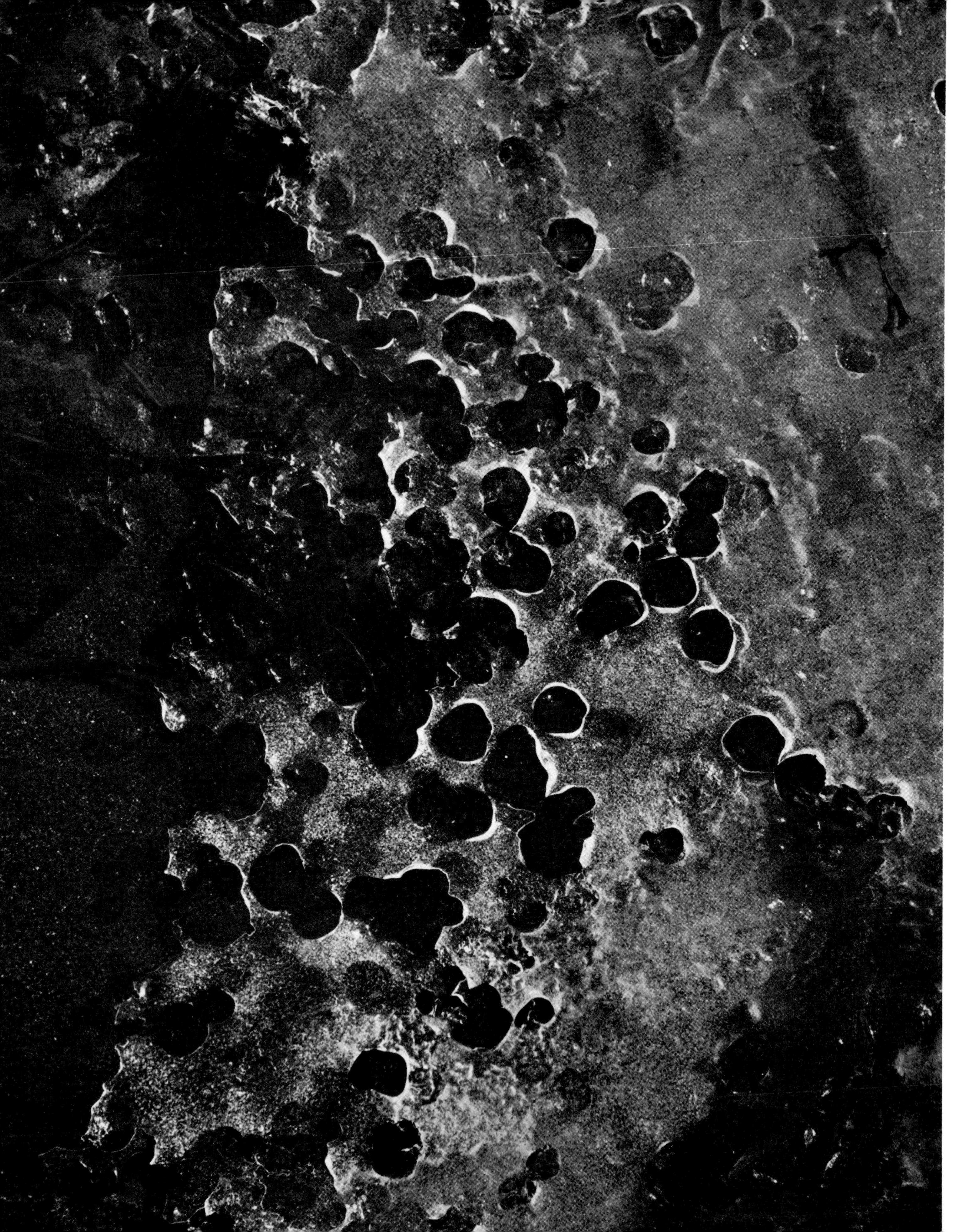

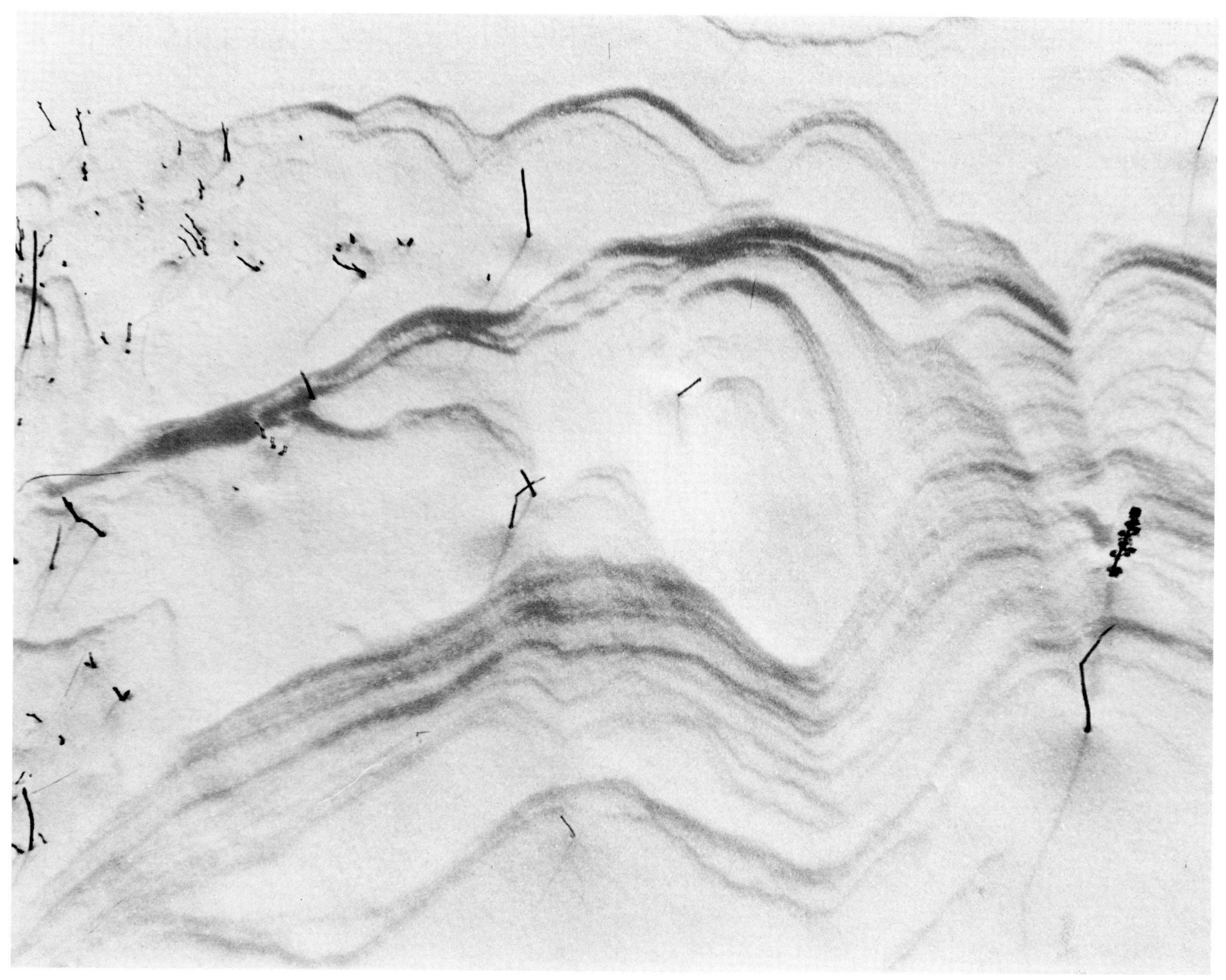

I searched along the edge of the sea for myself and found God instead.

It would be difficult to separate the people from their belief in God. Their faith is as rooted within them as are their communities on the granite ledges that compose the rugged coasts. They are not much for discussing complex theological concepts or prone to ponder weighty philosophical matters. Their faith is simple and it is organic to their way of life.

The coast people of Maine and eastern Canada are Christians, belonging to such denominations as Anglican, Baptist, Roman Catholic, Adventist, Presbyterian, Methodist, Congregational, United Church and others. In Maine, for example, most of the fishing folk are Protestant. In New Brunswick and Nova Scotia, there is a closer balance between Protestants and Roman Catholics, with French Acadians forming the largest portion of the latter. The Scots of Nova Scotia are both Presbyterian and Roman Catholic, the Highland Catholics having arrived in the province after the defeat of Bonnie Prince Charlie.

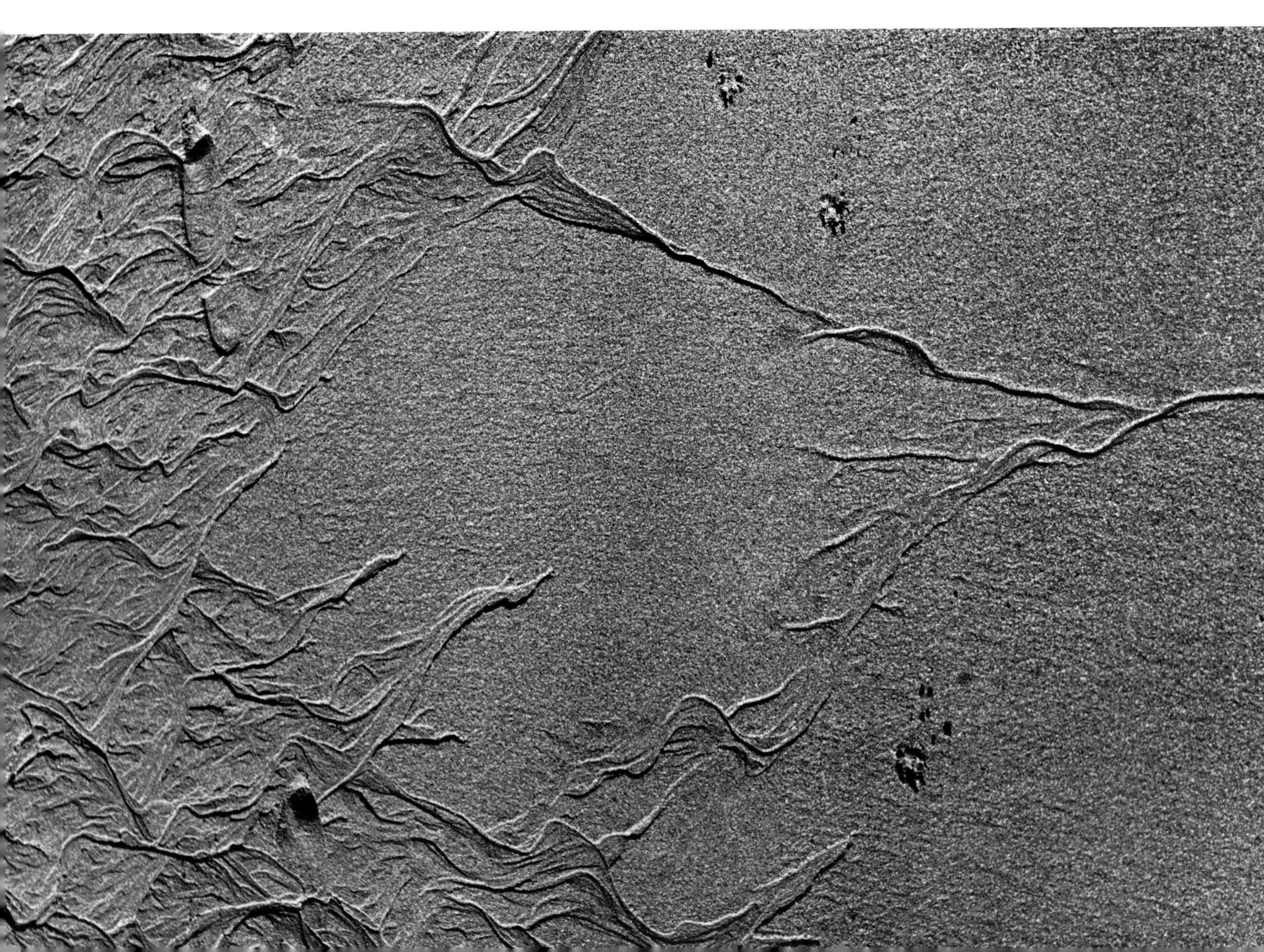

A priest in Canada tells his congregation not to be discouraged by the hardships of their way of life. He tells them that the Lord must have loved fishermen dearly because He chose His first Apostles from among them.

Above an isolated fishing village on the north coast of Quebec, an Anglican minister's airplane circles over the home of an elderly blind widow. He lands on an ice field and drives a snowmobile to her front door. Inside the warm house, the minister and the widow talk about many things that mean a great deal to both of them, particularly about people they love. He gently takes her worn hands in his and they pray together.

It is a simple service but it is how the coast people like their ministry, person to person.

Out of Bar Harbor, Maine, a minister sails his vessel, which he calls *God's Tugboat,* on journeys to the state's coastal and island communities, even as far out as Matinicus Rock. He brings the "good news" and fellowship in a way fishing people can understand.

In these seacoast communities, some continue working until they are seventy or eighty. They know almost everyone in their village and everyone knows them. While life for the old is lonely, they do not have to be alone and they are never abandoned. When the weather is warm, the old prefer to stay in their homes. But when the winter cold sets in or when some infirmity incapacitates them, the old move in with their grown children. However, some hardy souls continue to live in their homes, no matter what the weather, taking care of their chores — cleaning, chopping wood, cooking — until the day they die. Younger people address the old with respect, calling them Uncle or Auntie. Every age here has its place and no age is made to feel out of place.

It was a bright Sunday morning as I drove through a New Brunswick fishing village, west of St. Andrews. The cannery was shut down for the day and even the overwhelming odor of herring being processed into sardines seemed to be tolerable. On a slope of a hill, several levels of streets from the waterfront edge of the sardine cannery, stood a church with arched windows on its flanks and a sharp, pointed steeple commanding the front. I could hear the congregation singing the final strains of the recessional to the shrill notes of an off-key organ. The music stopped and I watched the people as they came out of the church into the summer sunlight. The children were delighted to be free from the constraints of parents and pews. They ran laughing, shouting, stirring up some drowsing gulls who squawked and quickly flew out of the way of rapidly approaching feet and anxious, grabbing hands. The old came out in clusters of widows and Sunday-best-suited gents. A young man helped his wife, who was bulging her yellow satin dress with a child near its time. They all passed the minister, who stood beaming and ramrod straight, shaking hands and exchanging talk of very little consequence, except to themselves.

On the Razor's Edge

I flew over a landscape that surely must have been that of the moon. But it was a petrified earth where the land and the sea were only distinguishable from each other by gray, white, purple, black, and blue gradations of frozen water. This was no land for every man. But, below me, the houses came into view, anchored to the ledges, safe from a cracking, breaking, grinding sea that was also ice.

In the winter, on the north coast of Quebec, every visual scene expresses the essence of cold, the deep green of spruce, the brilliance of snow and ice, the somber moods of the sea. Giant scars in the land are evidence of the great glaciers of the past. There is an almost absence of color during the day but at sunrise and sunset the shapes of the landscape absorb and reflect the warm reds, oranges, yellows, and purples of the sun's rays.

In the far northern areas of Quebec, Labrador, and Newfoundland, the fishing people live on a razor's edge, the void of the sea on one side and the desolate wilderness of the land on the other.

This is a harsh climate in winter. The days are often deceiving, with a clear sky and brilliant sun, causing the sea, rocks and the ice to reflect solar light like many highly polished mirrors. But the gusty winds and the subzero-degree temperatures act like swift, slashing swords, hacking at exposed flesh, making cheeks and noses feel like cracked slate shingles.

Those who hunt seals along this Quebec coast, in late autumn and early spring, do not kill them from helicopters or from factory ships but from small open boats, which because of their small capacity limits the number of seals taken and prevents wholesale slaughter. Seals contribute to the survival of the family and the community, providing both food and income. The existence of these communities depends on fishing for cod in the summer and hunting seals later in the year. If the people's right to hunt seals was eliminated, a main link in this chain of life would be gone and the communities would probably cease to exist.

Many of Quebec's English-speaking outport villages have schools which are taught by teachers from Canada, the United States, and Great Britain. It is not unusual for a young married couple, in the tiny settlement of Cross River in the north coast for example, to teach a total of seven grades. To continue their educations beyond the elementary or junior-high level, the children must leave their families and travel many hundreds of miles to the west to attend a school at Lennoxville, not far from Montreal, where they live with local families. This arrangement is a sacrifice for both parents and children, especially difficult for the young. They miss each other a lot but the parents are glad their children are getting the kind of education which was never available to them.

The late Dr. Wilfred Grenfell has become a legend to the people of northern Newfoundland, Labrador, and the north coast of Quebec. His work and that of his colleagues has continued to be realized through hospitals, doctors, nurses, specialists, medical services, and health programs for thousands of people who depend on the International Grenfell Association for life itself. The organization started with the vision of Dr. Grenfell, who committed himself and inspired others to serve the peoples of the north, the French and English-speaking whites, the Indians and the Eskimos. Today, these coastal villages are linked to each other by five hospitals, thirteen nursing stations, a children's dormitory, aircraft, a hospital ship, and a handicrafts center, all operated by the International Grenfell Association through its main center and hospital at St. Anthony, Newfoundland. The hospital and medical staff at Harrington Harbour, Quebec, is an example of this effort.

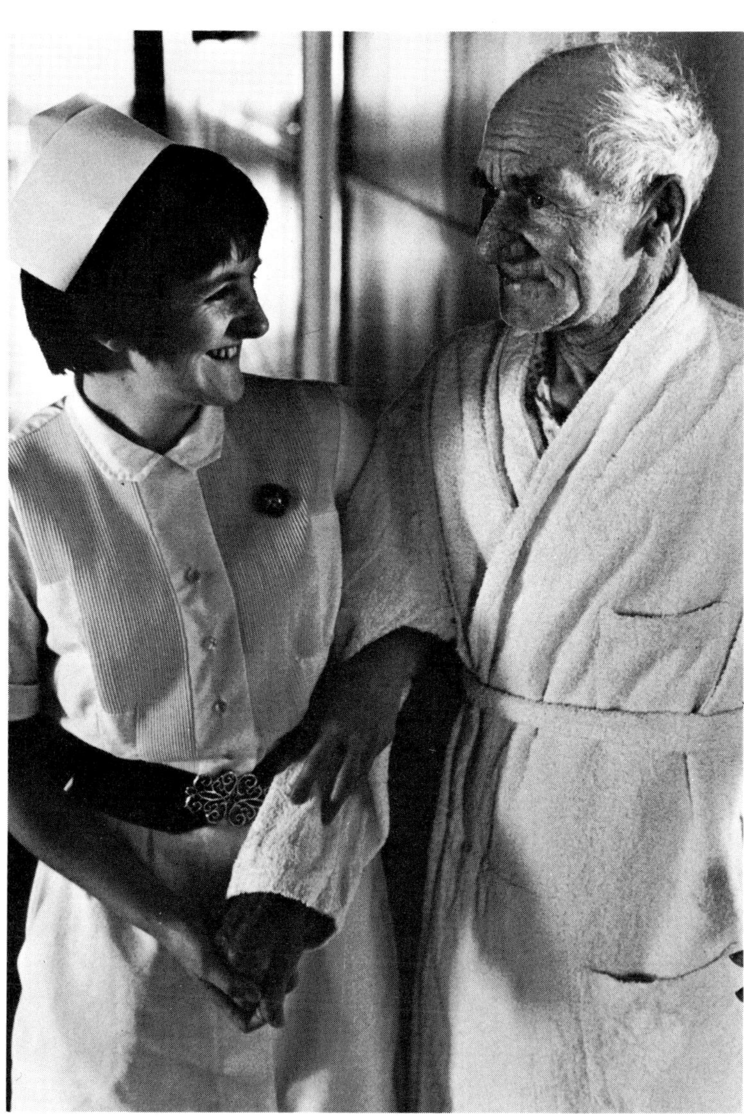

Time

I came upon an abandoned home in a grove of pines, not far from the shores of the Northumberland Strait. Near it, in an overgrown, forgotten meadow, there was a fishing boat, also unused and decaying. A raven lay dead, its wings flapping in a virile wind. This was all death and I wanted to feel life. Suddenly, snowbirds flitted out of the pines; their gyrations were swift dances from perch to air. A fisherman's child appeared next to me and said his name was Todd, loudly and proudly spelling it out for me: "T-O-D-D!"

ski-doo

In those villages where working the sea is still the way of life, one can walk and discover things that are there for some good purpose, such as grapnels still made of wood and stone and tied together with rope.

A glass jar of shark oil hangs suspended from the wood rafters in a Prospect Harbour, Nova Scotia, fishing shed. For fifteen years it has never failed to tell the correct direction of the wind. Everyone who lives on the edge of the sea is a watcher of the wind. "You've got to know what winds bring dirty weather and what ones bring fair," says one of the old-timers.

On a moody Cape Breton Island shore stands Fort Louisbourg, once built by Louis XIV to protect French interests in North American waters and the heartland of a new continent. It was taken by New Englanders and later leveled to the ground by the British. This fortified city rises anew, an ancient reminder of our imperial roots and the internationality of our maritime heritage.

The fleur-de-lis pierces the sky once more and the somber tower bell again rings the noon Angelus. No place on the coast of North America seems more lonely than this re-created symbol of our cultural pride and its own historical absurdity.

"A boat should always be in water. It looks unnatural resting there on the land. And when the paint peels off of her and the weeds grow around her and through her boards, it's like seeing a good friend who has died long ago and never was buried."

In Wiscasset, Maine, two old hulks, who were once proud sailing vessels, lie in mud banks, too much a reminder of the past to be destroyed and too far gone to be repaired.

"Those rotting guts have been out there so long that her good, strong keel has warped itself from the mud she's resting on. They were once the pride of the seas around here. They make me think of the old Bluenose schooners from Nova Scotia. You'd have to go a long way to match the sight of their beauty and speed. But those were different days. The people and their ways were different. Why, in those days, us maritime folk were the head of North America. Now it seems like we're the hind end. There's nothing left for that old lady to do but to just sit there and let the tide wash her bones away. I ain't against progress but what I really feel sorry about is that the kids today will never know what it was like, and, even if they did, they probably wouldn't care."

Along the coasts of Maine, New Brunswick, and Nova Scotia, one can find many houses where once people were born, lived, and died. Sometimes, when you look really closely, you can almost see these people.

I see a stove where countless meals were cooked, where a kettle was always kept going for tea, and where there was always a warm place to sit near in the winter. I see a mattress where overworked bodies were restored to peace in sleep and in death, and where a man and a woman's passion found each other and were satisfied. I see an ornate rocking chair, in what was once a parlor, where children rode stagecoaches, horses, and fantastic vehicles of their own invention, and where grandmothers thought mostly about the past. I see the old pictures, articles of clothing, broken furniture and stained papers, pieces of a puzzle that form the past lives of human beings.

Many of these former residents gave up and moved away from what was hard and poor to what they thought would be better. Some simply died, and there just was not anybody else to take their place. Most of the time, you feel the melancholy emptiness of the houses, brittle shells of wood and plaster. But, sometimes, there is a house which conveys a strong feel of something unseen, something imprisoned, something that does not want to be disturbed.

I see the wave in the distance as a total revolving unit, moving forward, coming nearer and growing larger. I feel it as it smashes against the granite land mass, disintegrating into a multitude of waterdrops catapulted in all directions. I feel the fierce gust of wind shearing through this volume of airborne water as it coalesces and transforms the sea into gobs of spume foam which spit out like cannon shot.

No Immunity from Change

In Canada, one village had several abandoned homes, wharfs, and sheds. Another village was supported by the government to be a living museum, showing visitors and tourists how a way of life used to be. In Maine, many of the towns have more homes belonging to outsiders than to the residents whose families have been there for generations, and other towns have expensive developments, selling lots at prices only the rich can afford, posting PRIVATE, NO TRESPASSING signs on a coast that once was accessible to all.

In both countries the edge of the sea is being subdivided, packaged, and sold to the highest bidder.

"It's pretty hard to satisfy what we want out of life just by fishing. The television shows us a lot of things we can have and our cars can take us to where we can get them. Maybe we'd be better off just being as we are, but it's pretty hard to resist some things when you think they'll make your life better."

"This is a tough, dangerous business, going for herring off the coast of New Brunswick. When the chips are down, like in a bad storm, the only thing you can really depend on are those things that have worked for you in the past. Poor judgment can mean the end of you and your crew. It's not that we're against progress, but we want to be sure that whatever new equipment or techniques we use will work. Anything less can mean disaster."

The dragger, with its sophisticated gear and long-range capability, is a technological improvement over the lone inshore fisherman, working out of his small boat. But the inshore fishermen say that while the draggers are more efficient, they are also indiscriminate in that they scoop up everything from the bottom, disturbing and even destroying an ecological balance.

"When we go out," one fisherman said, "we fish for whatever is in season, herring, cod, salmon, or what have you. But the draggers pull everything on board, tearing up the bottom and destroying the feeding grounds. They not only clean out the waters . . . but they clean us out as well."

In Machiasport and Searsport, Maine, and elsewhere, residents have discouraged the construction of oil refineries in their deep-water harbors. This response was brought about by a concern that oil might be spilled from an accident at such a facility or from the giant tankers that would deliver the crude oil.

In Arichat Harbour on Cape Breton Island, the tanker *Arrow* went down spilling over one and a half million gallons of crude oil and spoiling one of the most beautiful marine environments in North America.

"It seems just as we are getting our heads above water by solving one problem, such as getting more money for our catches, then something else comes along to knock us down again. This pollution business is pretty hard to fight. One day our fishing areas are clean and the next day a tanker goes down and that black crap is on everything. Sometimes, it seems like you just can't win."

An educational up-grading program is available for adults in many of Quebec's remote, north coastal settlements. This program functions in the winter when there is little or no activity in fishing or sealing. Those people who wish to participate are paid to attend classes in order to improve their language and mathematical skills, primarily on an elementary level. Those who favor the program say that the people who participate will be trained, through subsequent vocational courses, for new jobs more in demand by modern society than fishing. Opponents say that these are only "make-work" programs, just another form of welfare. They also say that even if people were retrained, they would have to leave their villages and seek work elsewhere. They wonder if their way of life no longer has any worth to society and if such programs represent a subtle way of destroying what has been a part of them for so long.

Their highway was once the sea and all the houses were built to face the water. Now asphalt cuts through the woods and makes its way by the back doors, bringing in strangers and pulling the people away.

To the young, the asphalt highway is a way out, an escape to something different.

There is something that the men can do to control their own economic lives. A significant number of inshore fishing men have become masters of their destiny by forming themselves into cooperatives, established within their own villages but linked to other similar groups for mutual economic benefit. Included in this cooperative organization are stores, credit unions, processing plants, and marketing outlets. The cooperative approach allows the men to retain their entrepreneurial status and to extend their power as individuals into those aspects of their economic life which were formerly controlled by others. Fishing co-ops can be found throughout the Canadian Maritimes, Quebec and Maine. The cooperative movement is now on an international scale in many areas of economic activity other than fishing. At Antigonish, Nova Scotia, the Coady International Institute is one of the intellectual centers for the world's cooperative movement. The institute trains local community leaders, representing every continent of the world, in the techniques of organizing and developing cooperatives.

Private interest groups and others who are against the cooperative movement sometimes charge it with being socialistic or communistic. But what these groups are really fighting is the extension of the prerogatives of free enterprise from the hands of a select few to those of the many.

In many fishing communities the organization of co-ops is extremely difficult because the men feel a sense of loyalty to the companies or individuals with whom they have been doing business for years, or they are reluctant to change their way of operating under any circumstances, even if this change would result in greater control over the economic forces that shape their lives. A well-managed and -administered cooperative may not be the total answer for preserving and strengthening their way of life but it can be an important part of the solution. Most important, it allows each man to actively participate in the ownership and management of those economic functions which were once used to exploit him.

"In the evening I look at the few boats floating out in the harbor in the moonlight . . . and I think to myself that it won't be long before they're all gone and the harbor will be empty."

"I like to go out fishing with my father. It's a lot of fun and I can earn a few extra bucks. I've learned a lot about the sea, boats, and about being a man from him. I like the sea but I don't want to spend the rest of my life there like my father. There's just no future to it. I know I'm not turning my back on my father because he tells me I'm right."

"I just can't wait until I'm old enough to leave this island. It's a great place when you're a little kid growing up. And when I'm married and have my own kids, this is just the kind of place I want to bring them up. There's no pollution. Most everybody is friendly. And you don't have to worry about some nut hurting you. But when you get older, well . . . it's different. It becomes the most boring place in the world because there's nothing to do. I just want to do more with my life . . . and that's why I can't wait to leave."

"I got out of here right after high school and hitchhiked to Montreal for a job. It didn't work out and then I went to Toronto. I worked in a factory and on the docks. I was good on the docks because I'm strong. I made some good money and bought a lot of things I never had before, like sharp clothes and a motorbike. I knew a few girls and almost got married to one of them. As hard as I tried to forget, I just couldn't get this place out of my mind. Maybe I was just homesick and couldn't get over it? Maybe I would have stayed away for good if I just learned how to forget? I suppose my real reason for coming back is that I thought I could be more myself here than some other place. Here . . . I'm with people I know . . . and I don't feel like a stranger or outsider. Now I'm working as a hand with one of the fishing crews and I've still got my motorbike. I hope to earn enough money to get married and get a boat and gear of my own. But for now it feels good just to be back home."

"I don't want my son to go into fishing for a living but I want him to study hard and I wouldn't mind it if he became something like a marine biologist. Then he could still be close to the sea but much better off than me."

BLAINE

A Catholic priest, from Shad Bay, Nova Scotia, who is the pastor of several fishing communities, foresees a possible loss not only for his own people but for all of contemporary society as well.

"When their way of work becomes more impersonal, less interdependent and neighborly, and once the risk and the sense of adventure is gone . . . their way of life will also be gone.

"But it hasn't come to that, yet. For the present, our whole society benefits from these people who still live close to nature and to each other. When and if they become totally assimilated into our contemporary society, all of us will have lost a vital part of our humanity, something that we can no longer go back to for those times when we desperately need a sense of peace and completeness."

The inshore fisherman, as an individual entrepreneur, has almost no future if he continues on his present course. However, by organizing himself into an effective and profitable cooperative, he has a good chance of revitalizing his way of life. This type of organization can serve as an economic, political, and social force to advance his self-interests. He needs newer and larger vessels that are equipped with electronic gear for finding fish and that are capable of going out farther and staying longer on the fishing grounds. With the help of advanced oceanographic research, he can discover new products to be harvested from the sea.

However, this task is impossible without the concern of American and Canadian society. The federal governments of both countries must take the responsibility and the obligation of providing their inshore fishermen with the money, tools, training, knowledge and protection they need to do the job. This commitment would not be a gift but an investment which would not only pay off in economic advantages but would, perhaps even more importantly, reinforce the philosophical structure on which these two unique nations have been built: the freedom of an individual to shape his own destiny, to contribute to society according to his own talents, and to enjoy the fruits of his labor.

Inshore fishing is one of the oldest occupations known to mankind. Through it a special way of life has developed in Maine and eastern Canada which has benefited many generations of people who work the sea and who live off their industry. The North American inshore fisherman is one man against the forces of nature — self-reliant, insular, strong, religious, and courageous. His way of life is being threatened as being unproductive, primitive, and an anachronism in today's world. His fishing areas have been depleted and polluted; his own methods have not kept pace with changing patterns of marine life, economics, and technology. He is rapidly being replaced by floating factory fishing systems which both catch and process their takes on the high seas. It is an irony that these fishing systems are not of his own country (the United States or Canada) but those of foreign competition, particularly the Soviet Union. While many countries protect their fishing industry by extending and enforcing their territorial waters up to 200 miles out from shore — Peru, for example — the North American governments offer indifference or tokenism at best.

Epilogue

There are many different kinds of worlds going on in our own. Take a good look at a whelk shell, for example, on the beach. There was once a creature who lived inside that shell. The tide washed it on shore and before long the gulls got at it and had a fine dinner for themselves. When you think about that shell, think about the world of the tide and the sea, the world of the shell and its creature, and the world of the gull and the sky. But that's only a small part of the many worlds we can see if we look with our hearts as well as our minds. Now look deeper into that shell and see how other creatures have carved designs on the inside. Some were born and died in that shell and never knew anything else. Look at the colors — the different purples, greens, whites, and browns. Take the shell and hold it at arm's length. Bring it forward a bit. Keep bringing it closer. Look at how the sunlight lets us see some things and hides others. The light changes, colors, and shows us new things about that shell all the time. And yet, that whelk shell is only one of many different shells, one of many different kinds of things constantly around us.

Our world of various peoples and their special ways is like the different shells on a beach. When they all exist, there is a great richness of diversity, some offering a greater sense of peace and beauty than others, all, nonetheless, are necessary to the spectrum of human life. If, one by one, they are removed or combined into one, we are left to ourselves and the loneliness of an empty beach.

Locations

d. Terence Bay, Nova Scotia
107. Old Fort, Quebec
108.a. Sambro area, Nova Scotia
b. Mount Desert Island, Maine
109. Prospect Harbour, Nova Scotia
110. Louisbourg, Nova Scotia
111. Bay of Fundy area, New Brunswick
112. Wiscasset, Maine
113. Northumberland Strait area, New Brunswick
114. Northumberland Strait area, New Brunswick
115. Peggy's Cove, Nova Scotia
116. Northumberland Strait area, New Brunswick
119. Mount Desert Island, Maine
120. Harrington Harbour, Quebec
121. Penobscot Bay, Maine
122. Peggy's Cove, Nova Scotia
124. Harrington Harbour, Quebec
125. Mount Desert Island, Maine
126. Terence Bay, Nova Scotia
128. Isle Madame, Nova Scotia
130. East Dover, Nova Scotia
131. Vinalhaven, Maine
132. Harrington Harbour, Quebec
133. Prospect Harbour, Nova Scotia
134. Terence Bay, Nova Scotia
137. Lubec, Maine
138. Mount Desert Island, Maine
140. Mount Desert Island, Maine